SIMPLE & TASTY SIDE DISHES

SIMPLE TASTY & SIDE DISHES

Frank R. Blenn

 American Diabetes Association®

Publisher	Editorial Director	Managing Editor
Susan H. Lau	Peter Banks	Christine B. Welch

Associate Editor	Director of Production
Sherrye Landrum	Carolyn S. Segree

Printed in the United States of America
99 98 97 96 95   10 9 8 7 6 5 4 3 2 1

American Diabetes Association
1660 Duke Street
Alexandria, VA 22314

Page design and typesetting services by Insight Graphics, Inc.
Cover design by Wickham & Associates, Inc.

Library of Congress Cataloging-in-Publication Data

Blenn, Frank R., 1963-
Simple & tasty side dishes / Frank R. Blenn.
p. cm. — (Healthy selects)
Includes index.
ISBN 0-945448-45-7
1. Diabetes—Diet therapy—Recipes. 2. Side dishes (Cookery)
I. Title. II. Title: Simple and tasty side dishes. III. Series.
RC662.B599 1995
641.5'6314—dc20   95-5678 CIP

CONTENTS

FOREWORD

The American Diabetes Association is proud to announce *Healthy Selects*, a new cookbook series dedicated to the premise that light, healthy food can be good for you *and* taste great, too. *Simple & Tasty Side Dishes*, the fifth book in the series, is a collection of easy-to-prepare side dish recipes you can serve at elegant parties or comfortable family dinners. Each recipe has American Diabetes Association–approved exchanges and all nutritional information provided. We know you'll enjoy the new ways to serve some of your favorite foods, as well as the unique ideas found in the series.

Author Frank Blenn created these recipes to help others cope with diabetes and thought to offer them to us in an effort to reach and assist a wider audience. We deeply appreciate his generosity. The Association owes a special debt of gratitude to Madelyn L. Wheeler, MS, RD, CDE, and her company, Nutritional Computing Concepts, for the thorough and careful preparation of nutritional calculations and exchange information. Ms. Wheeler offered many valuable suggestions through each step of the book production process. Robyn Webb Associates conducted taste-testing on every recipe and ensured the accuracy and quality of the finished product. Ms. Webb also developed many of the recipes in this book.

The original manuscript was reviewed by Karmeen Kulkarni, MS, RD, CDE, and Madelyn Wheeler, MS, RD, CDE. The final manuscript was reviewed by Sue McLaughlin, RD, CDE, and David B. Kelley, MD. Patty Walsh provided creative illustrations for each title in the series.

Have fun adding variety and zest to your diet with the *Healthy Selects* Series!

American Diabetes Association

PREFACE

Simple & Tasty Side Dishes is the fifth cookbook in a new series offering lighter and healthier recipes that still taste wonderful. I served many of these recipes, with great success, at elegant parties and casual dinners. I know you will appreciate the abundance of ways to serve the delicious recipes presented in this series.

My long-term goal was to write and share the results with you. With that in mind, I would like to offer my warmest and most sincere appreciation to the American Diabetes Association in helping me reach my goal. Without their interest and assistance, this series of books would just be another manuscript in my office.

I would like to dedicate this book to my family, who encouraged me to find a wider audience, and to my close friends (who are never without their opinions!) for taste-testing their way through many joyful times.

I hope you enjoy these delicious additions to a varied and healthy diet.

Frank R. Blenn

INTRODUCTION

Packed with tasty and easy-to-prepare recipes for vegetables, rice, and salads, *Simple & Tasty Side Dishes* is a terrific addition to your cookbook library. There are some important points to keep in mind, however, as you try all the recipes:

◆ The nutrient analysis section *only includes* the ingredients listed in the ingredients section. The nutrient analyses do *not* include serving suggestions sometimes provided in other sections of the recipe. For example, in the recipe for Vegetable-Stuffed Yellow Squash, we suggest that you add rice to the squash shells. But, because rice is not included as an ingredient, you know that the nutrient analysis only applies to the stuffed squash recipe itself. Similarly, suggested garnishes are not included in the analyses, unless they appear in the ingredients list.

◆ In general, we have suggested using olive oil instead of low-calorie margarine. You can use low-calorie margarine if you prefer, depending on your individual goals. Olive oil provides more monounsaturated fats, which are healthier, but low-calorie margarine does contain fewer calories. Feel free to interchange them if you need to.

◆ If you can find a version of an ingredient lower in fat than the low-fat items we used, feel free to use it instead. The recipes will still work, and your total fat grams will go down slightly. We usually use low-fat options, defined as containing 3 grams of fat or less per serving. When we use the term *low calorie,* that means 40 calories or less per serving. Lite soy sauce is lower in sodium than regular soy sauce. When we say a dash of salt, that's 1/16 of a teaspoon.

◆ In terms of nutrient values, 1 Starch/Bread Exchange can be interchanged with 1 Fruit Exchange.

◆ Note that the serving sizes in these recipes are not uniform and vary from recipe to recipe.

Good luck, and we hope you enjoy *Simple & Tasty Side Dishes.*

ADVENTUROUS VEGETABLES

CARROTS MARSALA

6 servings/serving size: 1/2 cup

*T*his side dish is so delicious you will want to serve this with an authentic Italian meal.

- ◆ **10 carrots (about 1 lb.), peeled and diagonally sliced**
- ◆ **1/4 cup Marsala wine**
- ◆ **1/4 cup water**
- ◆ **1 Tbsp. olive oil**
- ◆ **Fresh ground pepper**
- ◆ **1 Tbsp. fresh chopped parsley**

1. In a large saucepan, combine carrots, wine, water, oil, and pepper. Bring to a boil, cover, reduce the heat, and simmer for 10 minutes, basting occasionally.
2. Transfer to a serving dish, spoon any juices on top, and sprinkle with parsley.

Vegetable Exchange	1	Cholesterol	0 milligrams
Fat Exchange	1/2	Total Carbohydrate	7 grams
Calories	53	Dietary Fiber	2 grams
Total Fat	2 grams	Sugars	3 grams
Saturated Fat	0 grams	Protein	1 grams
Calories from Fat	21	Sodium	39 milligrams

DILL-FLAVORED CARROTS

6 servings/serving size: 1/2 cup

Oven-baked carrots that you can eat like French fries.

- **10 carrots (about 1 lb.), peeled and cut into sticks similar to French fries**
- **1 Tbsp. olive oil**
- **1/4 tsp. dried dill weed**
- **Fresh pepper**
- **1 Tbsp. water**

1. Place carrot sticks in the center of a large piece of aluminum foil. Add oil and sprinkle with dill weed, pepper, and water. Wrap carrots securely in foil, and crimp edges.
2. Bake at 375 degrees for 40 to 45 minutes or until carrots are tender.

....

Vegetable Exchange	1	Cholesterol	0 milligrams
Fat Exchange	1/2	Total Carbohydrate	6 grams
Calories	46	Dietary Fiber	2 grams
Total Fat	2 grams	Sugars	2 grams
Saturated Fat	0 grams	Protein	1 gram
Calories from Fat	21	Sodium	38 milligrams

GOLDEN VEGETABLE COMBO

8 servings/serving size: 1/2 cup

This dish with its bright color is a welcomed change from green vegetables.

- ◆ 1 cup sliced golden delicious apples, with skins
- ◆ 2 cups thinly sliced yellow squash
- ◆ 1-1/2 cups sliced carrots
- ◆ 1 small lemon, unpeeled, thinly sliced

- ◆ 2 tsp. cinnamon
- ◆ 1 Tbsp. golden raisins
- ◆ 1 tsp. nutmeg
- ◆ 1/2 cup water

1. Combine all ingredients in a saucepot, and cook over medium heat until carrots are tender, about 5 to 7 minutes. Serve.

....

Vegetable Exchange 1
Calories 31
Total Fat . . . . 0 grams
  Saturated Fat . . . . 0 grams
  Calories from Fat 0
Cholesterol . . . . 0 milligrams
Total Carbohydrate . . . . 8 grams
  Dietary Fiber . . . . 2 grams
  Sugars . . . . 5 grams
Protein . . . . 1 gram
Sodium . . . . 15 milligrams

VEGETABLE CONFETTI

8 servings/serving size: 1/2 cup

Everything but the kitchen sink is in here for a very nutritious side dish.

- ◆ 2 Tbsp. olive oil
- ◆ 1/2 cup plus 2 Tbsp. low-sodium chicken broth
- ◆ 1/4 cup chopped scallions
- ◆ 3 garlic cloves, minced
- ◆ 1 cup fresh broccoli, cut into florets
- ◆ 1 cup sliced zucchini
- ◆ 1 cup sliced mushrooms
- ◆ 1 cup cauliflower, broken into florets
- ◆ 3 medium potatoes, peeled and cubed
- ◆ 1 tsp. dried oregano
- ◆ 1/2 tsp. dried basil
- ◆ 1/2 tsp. dried thyme
- ◆ 1/4 tsp. paprika
- ◆ Fresh ground pepper

1. Heat olive oil and 2 Tbsp. of broth in a large skillet over medium heat. Add onions and garlic, and saute for 2 minutes.
2. Add vegetables and remaining broth. Cover and simmer for 15 to 20 minutes until vegetables are cooked but crisp. Sprinkle with dried herbs and pepper and serve.

....

Vegetable Exchange	2	Cholesterol	0 milligrams
Fat Exchange	1/2	Total Carbohydrate	10 grams
Calories	78	Dietary Fiber	2 grams
Total Fat	4 grams	Sugars	2 grams
Saturated Fat	1 gram	Protein	2 grams
Calories from Fat	33	Sodium	12 milligrams

GREEN BEANS WITH GARLIC AND ONION

6 servings/serving size: 1/2 cup

Great side dish for Chinese food.

- **1 lb. fresh green beans, trimmed and cut into 2-inch pieces**
- **2 Tbsp. olive oil**
- **1 small onion, chopped**
- **1 large garlic clove, minced**
- **1/4 cup white vinegar**
- **6 Tbsp. grated Parmesan cheese**
- **Fresh ground pepper**

1. Steam beans for 7 minutes or until just tender. Set aside.
2. In a skillet, heat oil over low heat. Add onion and garlic, and saute for 8 to 10 minutes or until onion is translucent. Transfer beans to a serving bowl and add onion mixture and vinegar, tossing well. Sprinkle with cheese and pepper and serve.

••

Vegetable Exchange	1	Cholesterol	4 milligrams
Fat Exchange	1-1/2	Total Carbohydrate	8 grams
Calories	97	Dietary Fiber	3 grams
Total Fat	6 grams	Sugars	2 grams
Saturated Fat	2 grams	Protein	4 grams
Calories from Fat	56	Sodium	96 milligrams

TANGY GREEN BEANS

6 servings/serving size: 1/2 cup

*P*ut some zing and zip into fresh green beans with this tasty side dish.

- 1 tsp. olive oil
- 1 large onion, chopped
- 1/2 cup chopped green pepper
- 1 lb. fresh green beans, trimmed
- 1 tsp. dried tarragon
- 1/4 cup water
- 1 tsp. lemon pepper

1. Add olive oil to a skillet, and saute onion until it is tender, about 5 or 6 minutes. Add green pepper, and saute for 5 minutes more.
2. Add green beans, tarragon, water, and lemon pepper, mixing well. Cover and simmer for 10 minutes or until beans are crisp yet tender. Transfer to a bowl and serve.

Vegetable Exchange 2
Calories 56
Total Fat . . . . 1 gram
   Saturated Fat . . . . 0 grams
   Calories from Fat 10
Cholesterol . . . . 0 milligrams
Total Carbohydrate . . . . 11 grams
   Dietary Fiber . . . . 3 grams
   Sugars . . . . 3 grams
Protein . . . . 2 grams
Sodium . . . . 4 milligrams

VEGETABLE-STUFFED YELLOW SQUASH

6 servings/serving size: 1 squash

A very filling side dish. Add rice to the bottom of the shells, and top with the vegetables for a meat-free meal.

- **6 small yellow squash**
- **1 tomato, finely chopped**
- **1/2 cup minced onion**
- **1/2 cup finely chopped green pepper**

- **1/2 cup shredded low-calorie cheddar cheese**
- **Fresh ground pepper**

1. Place squash in a large pot of boiling water. Cover, reduce heat, and simmer for 5 to 7 minutes or until squash is tender but firm. Drain and allow to cool slightly.
2. Trim stems from squash, and cut in half lengthwise. Gently scoop out the pulp, leaving a firm shell. Drain and chop the pulp.
3. In a large mixing bowl, combine pulp and the remaining ingredients, blending well.
4. Place squash shells in a 13x9x2-inch baking dish, gently spoon vegetable mixture into shells, and bake at 400 degrees for 15 to 20 minutes. Remove from oven and let cool slightly before serving.

....

Vegetable Exchange 2	Total Carbohydrate . . . . 8 grams
Calories 50	Dietary Fiber . . . . 2 grams
Total Fat . . . . 1 grams	Sugars . . . . 4 grams
Saturated Fat . . . . 0 grams	Protein . . . . 4 grams
Calories from Fat 10	Sodium . . . . 62 milligrams
Cholesterol . . . . 2 milligrams	

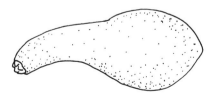

OVEN-FRIED YELLOW SQUASH

6 servings/serving size: 1/2 cup

Crunchy little morsels of golden goodness.

- 1/2 cup yellow cornmeal
- Fresh ground pepper
- 1 egg substitute equivalent
- 1 Tbsp. water
- 3 medium yellow squash, cut into 1/4-inch thick slices
- Nonstick cooking spray

1. Combine cornmeal and pepper. Mix thoroughly and set aside.
2. Combine egg and water. Dip each slice of squash into egg mixture and then cornmeal.
3. Lightly coat a 15x10x1-inch baking dish with cooking spray.
4. Place squash slices in a single layer, sprinkle remaining cornmeal on top, and bake at 450 degrees for 30 minutes or until golden brown, turning once. Transfer to a platter and serve.

....

Vegetable Exchange	1	Cholesterol	0 milligrams
Starch/Bread Exchange	1/2	Total Carbohydrate	12 grams
Calories	59	Dietary Fiber	2 grams
Total Fat	0 grams	Sugars	2 grams
Saturated Fat	0 grams	Protein	2 grams
Calories from Fat	0	Sodium	14 milligrams

BAKED SQUASH

6 servings/serving size: 1/2 cup

Southern-style squash that goes with any meal.

- ◆ **3 lb. yellow summer squash**
- ◆ **1/2 cup chopped onions**
- ◆ **2 egg substitute equivalents**
- ◆ **1/2 cup low-fat sour cream**
- ◆ **1 Tbsp. sugar**
- ◆ **1/2 tsp. salt (optional)**
- ◆ **Fresh ground pepper**
- ◆ **1/2 cup cracker meal**
- ◆ **2 tsp. olive oil**

1. Wash and slice squash into 1-inch rounds. Steam squash until tender.
2. In a large bowl, mash cooked squash, and mix with remaining ingredients except cracker meal and oil.
3. Place mixture into a casserole dish. Combine cracker meal and oil. Sprinkle over the casserole. Bake in a 375-degree oven for 1 hour or until brown on top.

....

Vegetable Exchange 1	Cholesterol . . . . 0 milligrams
Starch/Bread Exchange 1	Total Carbohydrate . . . . 19 grams
Fat Exchange 1/2	Dietary Fiber . . . . 3 grams
Calories 126	Sugars . . . . 10 grams
Total Fat . . . . 4 grams	Protein . . . . 5 grams
Saturated Fat . . . . 1 gram	Sodium . . . . 323 milligrams
Calories from Fat 38	w/o added salt . . . . . 131 milligrams

SQUASH AND TOMATO CASSOULET

6 servings/serving size: 1/2 cup

Squash and tomatoes combine in a smooth custard sauce.

- 1 Tbsp. olive oil
- 6 small yellow squash, sliced
- 1 medium onion, minced
- 2 garlic cloves, minced
- 2 Tbsp. chopped parsley
- Fresh ground pepper
- 2 medium tomatoes, sliced
- 4 egg substitute equivalents
- 1 cup skimmed evaporated milk

1. In a large skillet over medium heat, heat oil. Add squash, onion, and garlic and saute for 5 minutes. Add parsley and pepper.
2. Layer squash mixture and tomatoes in a casserole dish. Combine eggs with evaporated milk, blending well, and pour over vegetables. Bake at 350 degrees for 20 to 25 minutes or until custard is set. Remove from oven, and let cool slightly before serving.

....

Vegetable Exchange 2	Cholesterol . . . . 2 milligrams
Starch/Bread Exchange 1/2	Total Carbohydrate . . . . 15 grams
Fat Exchange 1/2	Dietary Fiber . . . . 2 grams
Calories 113	Sugars . . . . 10 grams
Total Fat . . . . 3 grams	Protein . . . . 8 grams
Saturated Fat . . . . 0 grams	Sodium . . . . 109 milligrams
Calories from Fat 26	

HERB-BROILED TOMATOES

4 servings/serving size: 1 tomato

Simple to fix, elegant to eat.

- ◆ **4 medium tomatoes**
- ◆ **1/4 cup grated Parmesan cheese**
- ◆ **2 Tbsp. plain dried bread crumbs**

- ◆ **2 Tbsp. fresh minced parsley**
- ◆ **1 tsp. dried basil**
- ◆ **1 tsp. dried oregano**
- ◆ **Fresh ground pepper**
- ◆ **1 Tbsp. olive oil**

1. Remove stems from tomatoes, and cut in half crosswise. Combine remaining ingredients in a small bowl, and lightly press mixture over cut side of tomato halves.
2. Place tomatoes on a baking sheet, cut side up, and broil about 6 inches from the heat for 3 to 5 minutes or until topping is browned.

Vegetable Exchange 2
Fat Exchange 1
Calories 95
Total Fat . . . . 6 grams
    Saturated Fat . . . . 2 grams
    Calories from Fat 80

Cholesterol . . . . 4 milligrams
Total Carbohydrate . . . . 9 grams
    Dietary Fiber . . . . 2 grams
    Sugars . . . . 4 grams
Protein . . . . 4 grams
Sodium . . . . 135 milligrams

MARINATED VEGETABLES

8 servings/serving size: 3/4 cup

*V*oila! Prepare this night before, and the next day indulge in a healthy bowl of garden-fresh vegetables.

- 4 medium carrots, peeled and diagonally sliced
- 1 small head cauliflower, broken into florets
- 2 small zucchini, sliced
- 1/4 lb. mushrooms, sliced
- 1 cup water
- 1 Tbsp. lemon juice
- 1 pkg. low-calorie salad dressing mix
- 1/3 cup white wine vinegar
- 1 small head butter lettuce leaves

1. Combine all vegetables except lettuce in a large bowl.
2. Combine water, lemon juice, salad dressing mix, and vinegar. Pour over vegetables, tossing well to coat. Cover and let marinate, refrigerated, overnight.
3. Just before serving, line a clear glass bowl with lettuce leaves, spoon vegetables into bowl, and serve chilled.

....

Vegetable Exchange	1	Total Carbohydrate	7 grams
Calories	31	Dietary Fiber	2 grams
Total Fat	0 grams	Sugars	4 grams
Saturated Fat	0 grams	Protein	2 grams
Calories from Fat	0	Sodium	169 milligrams
Cholesterol	0 milligrams		

CHINESE ASPARAGUS

4 servings/serving size: 1/2 cup

A delicious complement to any Chinese meal.

- 1 lb. asparagus
- 1/2 cup low-sodium chicken broth
- 2 Tbsp. lite soy sauce
- 1 Tbsp. rice vinegar
- 2 tsp. cornstarch
- 1 Tbsp. water
- 1 Tbsp. canola oil
- 2 tsp. grated ginger
- 1 scallion, minced

1. Trim the tough ends off the asparagus. Cut stalks diagonally into 2-inch pieces.
2. In a small bowl, combine broth, soy sauce, and rice vinegar.
3. In a measuring cup, combine cornstarch and water. Set aside.
4. Heat oil in a wok or skillet. Add ginger and scallions and stir-fry for 30 seconds. Add asparagus and stir-fry for a few seconds more. Add broth mixture and bring to a boil. Cover and simmer for 3 to 5 minutes until asparagus is tender.
5. Add cornstarch mixture and cook until thickened. Serve.

....

Vegetable Exchange 1	Cholesterol . . . . 0 milligrams
Fat Exchange 1	Total Carbohydrate . . . . 5 grams
Calories 60	Dietary Fiber . . . . 2 grams
Total Fat . . . . 4 grams	Sugars . . . . 2 grams
Saturated Fat . . . . 0 grams	Protein . . . . 2 grams
Calories from Fat 35	Sodium . . . . 313 milligrams

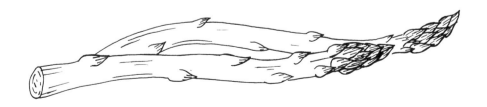

SHERRIED PEPPERS WITH BEAN SPROUTS

4 servings/serving size: 1/2 cup

This side dish has so many options: Add carrots, snow peas, or broccoli for more vegetables, or serve over rice or noodles or even a baked potato.

- ♦ **1 green pepper, julienned**
- ♦ **1 red pepper, julienned**
- ♦ **2 cups fresh bean sprouts**
- ♦ **2 tsp. lite soy sauce**
- ♦ **1 Tbsp. dry sherry**
- ♦ **1 tsp. red wine vinegar**

1. In a large skillet over medium heat, combine peppers, bean sprouts, soy sauce, and sherry, mixing well. Cover and cook for 5 to 7 minutes or until vegetables are just tender.
2. Stir in vinegar and remove from heat. Serve hot.

....

Vegetable Exchange	1	Total Carbohydrate	7 grams
Calories	33	Dietary Fiber	3 grams
Total Fat	0 grams	Sugars	1 gram
Saturated Fat	0 grams	Protein	2 grams
Calories from Fat	0	Sodium	109 milligrams
Cholesterol	0 milligrams		

SAUTEED SWEET PEPPERS

6 servings/serving size: 1/2 cup vegetables and about 1/3 cup rice

Add a little chicken or shrimp, and you can turn this side dish into a main meal.

- **2 medium green peppers, cut into 1-inch squares**
- **2 medium red peppers, cut into 1-inch squares**
- **1 Tbsp. olive oil**
- **2 Tbsp. water**
- **Fresh ground pepper**
- **1/2 tsp. dried basil**
- **2 cups precooked (1 cup uncooked) rice, hot**

1. In a large skillet over medium heat, heat oil. Add peppers and saute for 3 to 5 minutes, stirring frequently.
2. Add water and pepper; continue sauteing for 4 to 5 minutes or until peppers are tender. Stir in basil and pepper, and remove from heat.
3. Spread rice over a serving platter, spoon peppers and liquid on top, and serve.

Vegetable Exchange 1
Starch/Bread Exchange 1
Calories 110
Total Fat . . . . 3 grams
   Saturated Fat . . . . 0 grams
   Calories from Fat 23
Cholesterol . . . . 0 milligrams
Total Carbohydrate . . . . 20 grams
   Dietary Fiber . . . . 2 grams
   Sugars . . . . 2 grams
Protein . . . . 2 grams
Sodium . . . . 3 milligrams

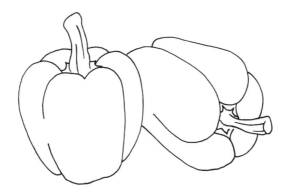

MULTICOLORED PEPPER STIR-FRY

4 servings/serving size: 1/2 cup

You can even use this dish as a base for adding chicken or shrimp. Place over noodles and then you have a main meal.

- 1 Tbsp. low-sodium chicken broth
- 2 medium carrots, cut into matchstick strips
- 1/2 cup each red, green, and yellow peppers, cored, seeded and sliced into matchstick strips
- 3/4 lb. snow peas, trimmed
- 2 Tbsp. lite soy sauce
- Fresh ground pepper

1. Heat broth in a large skillet. Add carrots and peppers and cook, covered, for 3 minutes.
2. Add snow peas, cover, and cook for 2 minutes. Add soy sauce and pepper and serve.

....

Vegetable Exchange 2
Calories 46
Total Fat . . . . 0 grams
   Saturated Fat . . . . 0 grams
   Calories from Fat 0
Cholesterol . . . . 0 milligrams

Total Carbohydrate . . . . 9 grams
   Dietary Fiber . . . . 3 grams
   Sugars . . . . 4 grams
Protein . . . . 2 grams
Sodium . . . . 324 milligrams

PARSLEY PEPPERS

6 servings/serving size: 1/2 cup

A colorful array of beautiful peppers.

- **2 slices Canadian bacon, cut into 1-inch pieces**
- **1 each large red, yellow, and green peppers, sliced into 1/4-inch strips**

- **1/4 tsp. dried oregano**
- **3 Tbsp. chopped parsley**

1. In a large skillet, saute bacon until crisp. Remove from skillet, reserving any drippings in skillet.
2. Add pepper strips and oregano to skillet. Saute peppers until tender, and stir in cooked bacon. Top with parsley and serve.

....

Vegetable Exchange 1
Fat Exchange 1/2
Calories 42
Total Fat . . . . 1 gram
   Saturated Fat . . . . 0 grams
   Calories from Fat 9
Cholesterol . . . . 6 milligrams
Total Carbohydrate . . . . 6 grams
   Dietary Fiber . . . . 2 grams
   Sugars . . . . 2 grams
Protein . . . . 3 grams
Sodium . . . . 150 milligrams

HERBED BROCCOLI

6 servings/serving size: 1/2 cup

Crunchy broccoli tossed with fresh herbs makes a fine side dish anytime.

- 3 cups water
- 1 lb. broccoli, cut into florets and stems sliced into coins
- 1 Tbsp. olive oil
- 1/4 cup minced onion

- 1 Tbsp. fresh chopped basil
- 1 tsp. fresh chopped oregano
- 1/2 tsp. fresh chopped thyme
- 2 tsp. grated fresh Parmesan cheese

1. Bring water to a boil in a large saucepot. Add broccoli, and cook for 3 minutes. Drain.
2. Place broccoli in a large bowl, and add the remaining ingredients. Toss well and serve.

....

Vegetable Exchange 1	Cholesterol . . . . 0 milligrams
Fat Exchange 1/2	Total Carbohydrate . . . . 4 grams
Calories 46	Dietary Fiber . . . . 2 grams
Total Fat . . . . 3 grams	Sugars . . . . 2 grams
Saturated Fat . . . . 0 grams	Protein . . . . 3 grams
Calories from Fat 24	Sodium . . . . 31 milligrams

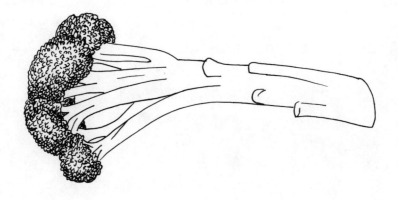

BROCCOLI WITH LEMON-BUTTER SAUCE

8 servings/serving size: 1/2 cup

Fresh broccoli only needs a little enhancement.

- ◆ **1-1/2 lb. fresh broccoli**
- ◆ **2 Tbsp. unsalted butter**
- ◆ **2 Tbsp. lemon juice**
- ◆ **1 large lemon, cut into wedges**

1. Wash broccoli, and trim tough stems. Cut each stalk of broccoli into several pieces.
2. Place broccoli into a vegetable steamer basket over boiling water. Cover and simmer for 10 minutes until broccoli is tender.
3. In a small skillet, melt butter, then add lemon juice. Drizzle lemon butter over broccoli, and serve with lemon wedges. Variation: For herbed broccoli, add 1/2 tsp. marjoram and 1/2 tsp. dried basil to the lemon-butter mixture.

Vegetable Exchange	1	Cholesterol	8 milligrams
Fat Exchange	1/2	Total Carbohydrate	4 grams
Calories	30	Dietary Fiber	2 grams
Total Fat	3 grams	Sugars	2 grams
Saturated Fat	2 grams	Protein	2 grams
Calories from Fat	30	Sodium	18 milligrams

HERBED BRUSSELS SPROUTS WITH CARROTS

4 servings/serving size: 1/2 cup

Serve this on Thanksgiving, and guests will plead for more.

- ◆ 3/4 lb. brussels sprouts
- ◆ 1/2 lb. baby carrots, peeled
- ◆ 2 cups low-sodium chicken broth
- ◆ 1 Tbsp. lemon juice
- ◆ 1/2 tsp. dried tarragon
- ◆ Dash nutmeg

1. Wash brussels sprouts well. In a medium saucepan, bring chicken broth to a boil. Add brussels and carrots, and return to a boil.
2. Cover, reduce heat, and simmer for 10 minutes. Remove from heat and drain.
3. Transfer vegetables to a serving bowl, and add lemon juice, tarragon, and nutmeg, tossing vigorously. Serve.

....

Vegetable Exchange 2	Total Carbohydrate . . . . 13 grams
Calories 67	Dietary Fiber . . . . 5 grams
Total Fat . . . . 1 grams	Sugars . . . . 5 grams
Saturated Fat . . . . 0 grams	Protein . . . . 4 grams
Calories from Fat 12	Sodium . . . . 73 milligrams
Cholesterol . . . . 1 milligram	

SNOW PEAS WITH SESAME SEEDS

6 servings/serving size: 1/2 cup

*A*lways make sure when you cook snow peas that the cooking time is only one minute. Snow peas should be bright green and very crisp.

- ◆ **2 cups water**
- ◆ **1 lb. trimmed fresh snow peas**
- ◆ **3 Tbsp. sesame seeds**
- ◆ **1 Tbsp. chopped shallots**
- ◆ **Fresh ground pepper**

1. Boil water in a saucepan. Add snow peas, and blanch one minute. Drain.
2. In a skillet, toast sesame seeds for 1 minute over medium heat. Add snow peas, shallots, and pepper. Continue sauteing for 1 to 2 minutes until snow peas are coated with sesame seeds. Serve.

....

Vegetable Exchange 1
Fat Exchange 1/2
Calories 56
Total Fat . . . . 2 grams
   Saturated Fat . . . . 0 grams
   Calories from Fat 22
Cholesterol . . . . 0 milligrams
Total Carbohydrate . . . . 6 grams
   Dietary Fiber . . . . 2 grams
   Sugars . . . . 3 grams
Protein . . . . 3 grams
Sodium . . . . 3 milligrams

ZUCCHINI AND ONION KABOBS

8 servings/serving size: 1/2 cup

A nice side dish for grilled fish, chicken, or beef.

- ◆ **6 medium zucchini (about 4 to 5 oz. each)**
- ◆ **4 medium red onions, quartered**
- ◆ **3/4 cup low-calorie Italian salad dressing**
- ◆ **3 Tbsp. lemon juice**
- ◆ **1 large lemon, cut into wedges**

1. Combine all ingredients in a large baking dish, mixing thoroughly. Cover and let marinate, refrigerated, for 2 to 3 hours. Remove vegetables from marinade (reserving marinade), and alternate zucchini and onion on skewers.
2. Grill kabobs 6 inches above medium heat, while basting frequently, for 20 minutes. Transfer to a platter, and garnish with lemon wedges. Serve with remaining marinade.

....

Vegetable Exchange 2		Total Carbohydrate . . . . 13 grams	
Calories 61		Dietary Fiber . . . . 2 grams	
Total Fat . . . . 1 gram		Sugars . . . . 9 grams	
Saturated Fat . . . . 0 grams		Protein . . . . 2 grams	
Calories from Fat 7		Sodium . . . . 324 milligrams	
Cholesterol . . . . 0 milligrams			

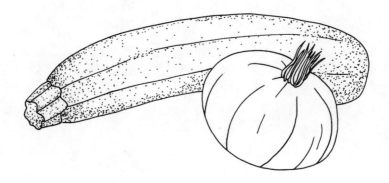

ZUCCHINI SAUTE

4 servings/serving size: 1/2 cup

*R*ed onion gives this zucchini a sweetness that is irresistible.

♦ 1 Tbsp. olive oil
♦ 1 medium red onion, chopped
♦ 3 medium zucchini (about 5 to 6 oz. each), cut into rounds
♦ 1/4 tsp. dried oregano
♦ Fresh ground pepper

1. In a large skillet over medium heat, heat oil. Add onion, and saute until onion is translucent but not browned.
2. Add zucchini, cover, and simmer 3 to 4 minutes. Sprinkle with oregano and pepper, and serve hot.

....

Vegetable Exchange 1
Fat Exchange 1
Calories 62
Total Fat . . . . 3 grams
  Saturated Fat . . . . 0 grams
  Calories from Fat 31
Cholesterol . . . . 0 milligrams
Total Carbohydrate . . . . 8 grams
  Dietary Fiber . . . . 2 grams
  Sugars . . . . 5 grams
Protein . . . . 1 gram
Sodium . . . . 4 milligrams

ARTICHOKE PARMESAN

4 servings/serving size: 1/2 cup

These tender hearts with crumb topping are as easy as they are elegant.

- **1/4 cup plain dried bread crumbs**
- **2 Tbsp. Parmesan cheese**
- **4 Tbsp. low-calorie Italian salad dressing**
- **9 oz. canned and drained (packed in water) or frozen and thawed artichoke hearts**
- **2 medium tomatoes, quartered**

1. In a small bowl, combine bread crumbs, cheese, and 3 Tbsp. salad dressing. Mix well and set aside.
2. In another bowl, combine artichoke hearts with remaining 1 Tbsp. salad dressing, tossing thoroughly. Arrange artichoke hearts and tomato wedges in a 1-qt. casserole dish.
3. Sprinkle bread crumb mixture over vegetables, and bake at 350 degrees for 35 to 40 minutes or until topping is light brown.

Vegetable Exchange	1	Cholesterol	2 milligrams
Starch/Bread Exchange	1/2	Total Carbohydrate	14 grams
Fat Exchange	1/2	Dietary Fiber	12 grams
Calories	83	Sugars	8 grams
Total Fat	2 grams	Protein	4 grams
Saturated Fat	1 gram	Sodium	352 milligrams
Calories from Fat	18		

CREOLE EGGPLANT

6 servings/serving size: 1/2 cup

Instead of frying eggplant, dress it up in a tangy Creole sauce.

- 1 medium (4-oz.) eggplant
- 2 medium garlic cloves, minced
- 1 large green bell pepper, chopped
- 1 medium onion, chopped
- 1/4 tsp. dried thyme
- 1/4 tsp. dried rosemary
- Dash hot pepper sauce (or to taste)
- 1/4 tsp. chili powder
- 10 oz. no-salt-added tomato sauce

1. Peel and cube eggplant. Place in a bowl of salted water (1/2 tsp.) to cover, and let eggplant stand for 1 hour. Drain and pat dry.
2. Combine all ingredients in a large skillet over low heat, mixing well. Cover and simmer for 15 to 20 minutes until vegetables are tender. Transfer to a serving dish and serve.

Vegetable Exchange	2	Total Carbohydrate	10 grams
Calories	42	Dietary Fiber	2 grams
Total Fat	0 grams	Sugars	5 grams
Saturated Fat	0 grams	Protein	2 grams
Calories from Fat	0	Sodium	12 milligrams
Cholesterol	0 milligrams		

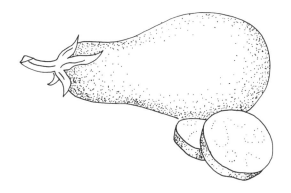

CREAMED SPINACH

4 servings/serving size: 1/2 cup

A *family favorite.*

- ◆ 1-1/2 lb. fresh spinach leaves
- ◆ 2 Tbsp. low-calorie margarine
- ◆ 2 Tbsp. cornstarch
- ◆ Fresh ground pepper

- ◆ Dash salt
- ◆ 3/4 cup evaporated skim milk
- ◆ 1 egg substitute equivalent, beaten

1. Remove and discard tough spinach stems. Wash leaves thoroughly and chop. Steam the spinach for 3 to 5 minutes, and set aside.
2. In a skillet, heat margarine. Blend in cornstarch and pepper and salt. Stir constantly.
3. Add milk, bring to a boil, and stir constantly for 1 minute. Remove sauce from heat.
4. Vigorously stir about 3 Tbsp. sauce into the beaten egg and immediately add this mixture back to the skillet. Add steamed spinach to the skillet and coat with sauce. Serve.

....

Starch/Bread Exchange 1	Cholesterol .... 2 milligrams
Fat Exchange 1/2	Total Carbohydrate .... 13 grams
Calories 105	Dietary Fiber .... 2 grams
Total Fat .... 3 grams	Sugars .... 5 grams
Saturated Fat .... 1 gram	Protein .... 8 grams
Calories from Fat 28	Sodium .... 219 milligrams

TURNIP AND POTATO PUREE

6 servings/serving size: about 1/2 cup

Turnips turn into something special when paired with potatoes with a slightly sweet taste.

- 1 lb. turnips, peeled and cubed
- 1/2 lb. russet potatoes, peeled and cubed
- 1/4 cup orange juice
- 2 Tbsp. fructose
- 1/2 tsp. grated fresh ginger
- 2 tsp. low-calorie margarine
- Fresh ground pepper

1. In a medium saucepot, cook turnips and potatoes in boiling water to cover until tender, about 15 to 20 minutes. Drain.
2. Transfer vegetables to a food processor. Puree until smooth.
3. Return vegetables to saucepot, and add remaining ingredients. Cook over low heat for 5 minutes. Serve.

....

Vegetable Exchange 1	Cholesterol . . . . 0 milligrams
Starch/Bread Exchange 1/2	Total Carbohydrate . . . . 13 grams
Calories 58	Dietary Fiber . . . . 2 grams
Total Fat . . . . 1 gram	Sugars . . . . 6 grams
Saturated Fat . . . . 0 grams	Protein . . . . 1 gram
Calories from Fat 7	Sodium . . . . 40 milligrams

ORANGE-GLAZED BEETS

4 servings/serving size: 1/2 cup

This is a nice side dish for the holidays.

- 3/4 cup unsweetened orange juice
- 1 Tbsp. cornstarch
- 1/2 tsp. orange rind
- 1/4 tsp. ginger
- 16 oz. canned sliced beets, drained

1. In a large skillet over medium heat, combine orange juice, cornstarch, orange rind, and ginger.
2. Add beets and bring to a boil. Continue cooking for 1 to 2 minutes or until sauce thickens, stirring constantly. Transfer to a serving dish, spoon sauce on beets, and serve.

....

Vegetable Exchange 1
Fruit Exchange 1/2
Calories 52
Total Fat . . . . 0 grams
   Saturated Fat . . . . 0 grams
   Calories from Fat 0
Cholesterol . . . . 0 milligrams
Total Carbohydrate . . . . 12 grams
   Dietary Fiber . . . . 1 gram
   Sugars . . . . 9 grams
Protein . . . . 1 gram
Sodium . . . . 210 milligrams

MUSHROOMS IN GARLIC BUTTER

6 servings/serving size: 1/2 cup

A pleasant combination of mushrooms and red onion.

- ◆ 2 Tbsp. olive oil
- ◆ 1 garlic clove, minced
- ◆ 1/4 cup white vinegar
- ◆ Fresh ground pepper
- ◆ 1 lb. mushrooms, sliced
- ◆ 1 small red onion, thinly sliced and separated into rings
- ◆ 2 Tbsp. chopped parsley

1. In a large skillet, heat oil and saute garlic for 2 minutes. Stir in vinegar and pepper.
2. Add mushrooms and onion rings, cover, and steam for 10 minutes. Uncover and let cook for 5 more minutes. Remove from heat and add parsley.

Vegetable Exchange 1
Fat Exchange 1
Calories 62
Total Fat . . . . 5 grams
    Saturated Fat . . . . 1 gram
    Calories from Fat 43
Cholesterol . . . . 0 milligrams
Total Carbohydrate . . . . 5 grams
    Dietary Fiber . . . . 1 gram
    Sugars . . . . 2 grams
Protein . . . . 1 gram
Sodium . . . . 2 milligrams

MUSHROOM CASSOULETS

6 servings/serving size: 1/2 cup

*H*ere is a side dish that is not a bit of trouble to prepare, yet tastes expensive, and everyone will think you worked all day to make it.

* 1 lb. mushrooms, sliced
* 1 medium onion, chopped
* 1 cup low-sodium chicken broth
* 1 sprig thyme
* 1 sprig oregano
* 1 stalk of celery leaves
* 2 Tbsp. lemon juice
* Fresh ground pepper
* 1/2 cup dried bread crumbs
* 2 Tbsp. olive oil

1. Combine mushrooms, onion, and chicken broth in a saucepan. Tie together thyme, oregano, and celery leaves and add to mushrooms.
2. Add lemon juice and pepper, and bring to a boil. Boil until liquid is reduced, about 10 minutes.
3. Divide mushroom mixture equally into small ramekins. Mix bread crumbs and oil together, and sprinkle on top of each casserole.
4. Bake at 350 degrees for 20 minutes or until tops are golden brown. Remove from heat, and let cool slightly before serving.

Vegetable Exchange 1
Starch/Bread Exchange 1/2
Fat Exchange 1
Calories 106
Total Fat . . . . 6 grams
  Saturated Fat . . . . 1 gram
  Calories from Fat 50
Cholesterol . . . . 0 milligrams
Total Carbohydrate . . . . 12 grams
  Dietary Fiber . . . . 2 grams
  Sugars . . . . 3 grams
Protein . . . . 3 grams
Sodium . . . . 88 milligrams

MOCK HOLLANDAISE

4 servings/serving size: 2 Tbsp.

Use over any fresh, lightly steamed vegetable.

- **1/2 cup low-calorie low-fat mayonnaise**
- **3 Tbsp. water**
- **1 Tbsp. lemon juice**
- **Fresh white pepper**

1. In a small saucepan, combine all ingredients. Whisk until smooth.
2. Simmer mixture over low heat, stirring constantly, for 3 to 4 minutes, until heated through.

....

Fat Exchange	2	Total Carbohydrate	2 grams
Calories	101	Dietary Fiber	0 grams
Total Fat	9 grams	Sugars	1 gram
Saturated Fat	1 gram	Protein	0 grams
Calories from Fat	83	Sodium	221 milligrams
Cholesterol	12 milligrams		

REMARKABLE RICE

VEGETABLE RICE

4 servings/serving size: about 1/2 cup

*V*ary this dish with whatever you have on hand.

- ◆ 1 Tbsp. olive oil
- ◆ 1/4 cup chopped red onion
- ◆ 1 cup low-sodium chicken broth
- ◆ 1 cup uncooked rice

- ◆ 1/4 cup dry white wine
- ◆ 2 small carrots, peeled and sliced thin
- ◆ 1/4 cup minced green pepper
- ◆ Fresh ground pepper

1. In a skillet, heat oil. Add onion and saute for 5 minutes.
2. Add broth, rice, and wine. Bring to a boil, cover, and simmer for 15 minutes.
3. Stir in carrots and green pepper. Simmer an additional 10 minutes until rice is tender and liquid is absorbed. Transfer to a serving bowl and serve. Variations: Add 1 cup broccoli florets, 1/2 cup chopped red pepper, 1/2 cup cooked peas, or 1 cup cauliflower florets along with the carrots.

Starch/Bread Exchange	3	Total Carbohydrate	41 grams
Calories	226	Dietary Fiber	1 gram
Total Fat	4 grams	Sugars	2 grams
Saturated Fat	1 gram	Protein	4 grams
Calories from Fat	37	Sodium	31 milligrams
Cholesterol	0 milligrams		

ORIENTAL FRIED RICE

4 servings/serving size: 1/2 cup

A favorite you can make at home.

- ◆ 2 Tbsp. peanut oil
- ◆ 1/4 cup chopped onion
- ◆ 1/2 cup sliced carrot
- ◆ 2 Tbsp. chopped green pepper
- ◆ 2 cups cooked rice
- ◆ 1/2 cup water chestnuts, drained

- ◆ 1/2 cup sliced mushrooms
- ◆ 2 Tbsp. lite soy sauce
- ◆ 3 egg substitute equivalents, beaten
- ◆ 1/2 cup sliced scallions

1. In a large skillet, heat oil. Saute onion, carrot, and green pepper for 5 to 6 minutes.
2. Stir in rice, water chestnuts, mushrooms, and soy sauce, and continue to cook for 8 to 10 minutes.
3. Stir in eggs, and continue to cook for another 3 minutes. Top with sliced scallions to serve.

....

Starch/Bread Exchange 2
Fat Exchange 1
Calories 217
Total Fat . . . . 7 grams
    Saturated Fat . . . . 1 gram
    Calories from Fat 66

Cholesterol . . . . 0 milligrams
Total Carbohydrate . . . . 31 grams
    Dietary Fiber . . . . 2 grams
    Sugars . . . . 4 grams
Protein . . . . 7 grams
Sodium . . . . 377 milligrams

CURRIED RICE WITH PINEAPPLE

4 servings/serving size: about 1/2 cup

Sweet pineapple sparks the flavor in this side dish.

- 1 onion, chopped
- 1-1/2 cups water
- 1-1/4 cups low-sodium beef broth
- 1 cup uncooked rice

- 1 tsp. curry powder
- 1/4 tsp. garlic powder
- 8 oz. pineapple chunks, drained

1. In a medium saucepan, combine onion, water, and beef broth. Bring to a boil, and add rice, curry powder, and garlic powder. Cover and reduce heat. Simmer for 25 minutes.
2. Add pineapple and continue to simmer 5 to 7 minutes more until rice is tender and water is absorbed. Transfer to a serving bowl and serve.

Starch/Bread Exchange 3
Calories 215
Total Fat . . . . 1 gram
   Saturated Fat . . . . 0 grams
   Calories from Fat 8
Cholesterol . . . . 0 milligrams

Total Carbohydrate . . . . 46 grams
   Dietary Fiber . . . . 2 grams
   Sugars . . . . 7 grams
Protein . . . . 5 grams
Sodium . . . . 21 milligrams

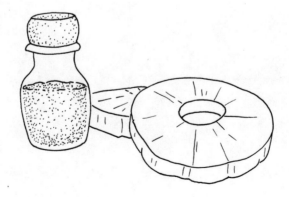

BROWN RICE
WITH MUSHROOMS

6 servings/serving size: 1/2 cup

Instead of the usual white rice, try to include brown rice in your meals. Along with a nutty taste, it packs some fiber and vitamins.

- ◆ 1 tsp. olive oil
- ◆ 1/2 cup chopped scallions
- ◆ 2 cups sliced mushrooms
- ◆ 3 cups cooked brown rice
- ◆ 2 Tbsp. chopped parsley
- ◆ Paprika

1. In a large skillet over medium heat, heat oil. Add scallions and mushrooms, and saute for 4 minutes.
2. Add rice, stirring frequently, until heated through.
3. Remove from heat, stir in parsley, and sprinkle with paprika.

Starch/Bread Exchange 1-1/2
Calories 128
Total Fat .... 2 grams
    Saturated Fat .... 0 grams
    Calories from Fat 17
Cholesterol .... 0 milligrams
Total Carbohydrate .... 25 grams
    Dietary Fiber .... 3 grams
    Sugars .... 1 gram
Protein .... 3 grams
Sodium .... 8 milligrams

CONFETTI RICE

4 servings/serving size: about 1/2 cup

*S*peckles of pimento add interest to this side dish.

- 1 Tbsp. olive oil
- 1/2 cup sliced mushrooms
- 1 garlic clove, minced
- 1-1/2 cups low-sodium chicken broth
- Fresh ground pepper
- 1 Tbsp. chopped parsley
- 2 oz. diced pimentos, drained
- 1/2 cup sliced water chestnuts
- 1 cup uncooked rice

1. In a skillet, heat oil. Add mushrooms and garlic, and saute for 5 minutes. Add broth and pepper, and bring to a boil.
2. Add parsley, pimentos, water chestnuts, and rice. Cover, reduce heat, and simmer for 20 to 25 minutes or until rice is tender and liquid is absorbed. Transfer to a serving bowl.

....

Starch/Bread Exchange	3	Total Carbohydrate	41 grams
Calories	227	Dietary Fiber	1 gram
Total Fat	4 grams	Sugars	2 grams
Saturated Fat	1 gram	Protein	5 grams
Calories from Fat	39	Sodium	25 milligrams
Cholesterol	0 milligrams		

ONION-SEASONED RICE

4 servings/serving size: about 1/2 cup

Calling all onion lovers.

- ◆ 1 Tbsp. olive oil
- ◆ 2 onions, finely chopped
- ◆ 1 cup uncooked rice
- ◆ 1-1/4 cups low-sodium chicken broth

- ◆ 3/4 cup water
- ◆ 1 Tbsp. Worcestershire sauce
- ◆ Fresh ground pepper
- ◆ 2 Tbsp. minced parsley

1. In a large skillet, heat oil. Add onion, and saute for 5 to 7 minutes.
2. Add rice, broth, water, Worcestershire sauce, and pepper. Bring to a boil.
3. Transfer mixture to a casserole dish, and bake at 350 degrees for 50 minutes. Garnish with parsley.

Starch/Bread Exchange 3
Calories 250
Total Fat . . . . 4 grams
   Saturated Fat . . . . 1 gram
   Calories from Fat 39
Cholesterol . . . . 0 milligrams

Total Carbohydrate . . . . 47 grams
   Dietary Fiber . . . . 2 grams
   Sugars . . . . 5 grams
Protein . . . . 5 grams
Sodium . . . . 61 milligrams

RICE AND PEAS ITALIANO

6 servings/serving size: 1/2 to 3/4 cup

In Italian, this is called Risi e Bisi. *Rice and peas go together so well.*

- **2 Tbsp. olive oil**
- **1/2 cup minced onion**
- **1 garlic clove, minced**
- **1 cup uncooked rice**
- **1 tsp. fresh oregano**
- **2 cups low-sodium chicken broth**
- **2 cups cooked green peas**
- **2 Tbsp. Parmesan cheese**
- **Fresh ground pepper**

1. In a saucepan, heat oil. Add onion and garlic, and saute for 5 minutes.
2. Add rice and oregano, and saute for 2 minutes more. Add broth, and bring to a boil. Reduce heat, cover, and simmer for 15 minutes.
3. Transfer to a bowl, and add remaining ingredients.

Starch/Bread Exchange 2
Fat Exchange 1
Calories 219
Total Fat . . . . 6 grams
 Saturated Fat . . . . 1 gram
 Calories from Fat 53
Cholesterol . . . . 2 milligrams
Total Carbohydrate . . . . 34 grams
 Dietary Fiber . . . . 3 grams
 Sugars . . . . 4 grams
Protein . . . . 7 grams
Sodium . . . . 98 milligrams

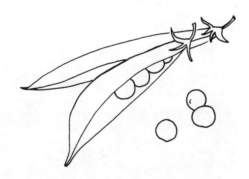

SAUTEED RICE WITH HERBS

4 servings/serving size: about 1/2 cup

*T*ry this side dish with turkey or chicken.

- ◆ **1 Tbsp. olive oil**
- ◆ **1 cup uncooked rice**
- ◆ **1 cup chopped onion**
- ◆ **1 tsp dried rosemary**

- ◆ **1/2 tsp. dried savory**
- ◆ **1/2 tsp. dried marjoram**
- ◆ **2-1/4 cups low-sodium chicken broth**

1. In a skillet, heat oil. Add rice and onion, and saute for 5 to 7 minutes.
2. Stir in remaining ingredients, and bring to a boil. Cover, reduce heat, and simmer for 20 to 25 minutes until liquid is absorbed. Transfer to a serving bowl and serve.

....

Starch/Bread Exchange 3
Calories 235
Total Fat . . . . 5 grams
   Saturated Fat . . . . 1 gram
   Calories from Fat 42
Cholesterol . . . . 1 milligram

Total Carbohydrate . . . . 42 grams
   Dietary Fiber . . . . 1 gram
   Sugars . . . . 3 grams
Protein . . . . 5 grams
Sodium . . . . 35 milligrams

COLORFUL RICE CASSEROLE

12 servings/serving size: 1/4 cup rice plus 1/2 cup vegetables

Use this recipe when zucchini are at their best.

- 1 Tbsp. olive oil
- 1-1/2 lb. zucchini, thinly sliced
- 3/4 cup chopped scallions
- 2 cups corn kernels (frozen or fresh; if frozen, defrost)
- 16-oz. can no-salt-added coarsely chopped tomatoes, undrained
- 1/4 cup chopped parsley
- 1 tsp. oregano
- 3 cups cooked rice (white or brown)

1. In a large skillet, heat oil. Add zucchini and scallions, and saute for 5 minutes.
2. Add remaining ingredients, cover, reduce heat, and simmer for 10 to 15 minutes or until vegetables are heated through. Transfer to a bowl and serve.

....

Starch/Bread Exchange 1	Cholesterol .... 0 milligrams	
Vegetable Exchange 1	Total Carbohydrate .... 23 grams	
Calories 108	Dietary Fiber .... 3 grams	
Total Fat .... 1 gram	Sugars .... 5 grams	
Saturated Fat .... 0 grams	Protein .... 3 grams	
Calories from Fat 12	Sodium .... 106 milligrams	

RICE PARMESAN

4 servings/serving size: about 1/2 cup

You can probably make this dish anytime with ingredients you have on hand.

- 1 Tbsp. olive oil
- 1 medium onion, chopped
- 1 garlic clove, minced
- 1 cup low-sodium chicken broth
- 1 cup uncooked rice
- 1/2 cup dry white wine
- 1/2 cup grated Parmesan cheese

1. In a skillet over medium heat, heat oil. Add onion and garlic, and saute for 8 minutes.
2. Stir in chicken broth, rice, and wine, and bring to a boil. Reduce heat to low, cover, and continue cooking for 20 to 25 minutes or until liquid is absorbed. Transfer to a serving bowl, and add cheese before serving.

Starch/Bread Exchange	3	Cholesterol	8 milligrams
Fat Exchange	1	Total Carbohydrate	42 grams
Calories	279	Dietary Fiber	1 gram
Total Fat	7 grams	Sugars	4 grams
Saturated Fat	3 grams	Protein	9 grams
Calories from Fat	64	Sodium	204 milligrams

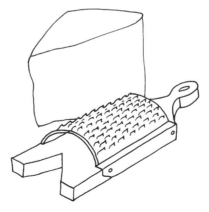

RICE WITH SPINACH AND FETA CHEESE

6 servings/serving size: 1/3 cup

*R*ice with a Greek twist.

- 1 cup uncooked rice
- 1 cup low-sodium chicken broth
- 1 cup water
- 1 Tbsp. olive oil
- 1 medium onion, chopped
- 1 cup sliced mushrooms
- 2 garlic cloves, minced
- 1 Tbsp. lemon juice
- 1/2 tsp. dried oregano
- 6 cups fresh spinach, stems trimmed, washed, patted dry, and coarsely chopped
- 4 oz. feta cheese, crumbled
- Fresh ground pepper

1. In a medium saucepan over medium heat, combine rice, chicken broth, and water. Bring to a boil, cover, reduce heat, and simmer for 15 minutes. Transfer to a serving bowl.
2. In a skillet, heat oil. Saute onion, mushrooms, and garlic for 5 to 7 minutes. Stir in lemon juice and oregano. Add spinach, cheese, and pepper, tossing until spinach is slightly wilted. Toss with rice and serve.

....

Starch/Bread Exchange	2	Cholesterol	17
Fat Exchange	1	Total Carbohydrate	32 grams
Calories	219	Dietary Fiber	3 grams
Total Fat	7 grams	Sugars	3 grams
Saturated Fat	3 grams	Protein	8 grams
Calories from Fat	64	Sodium	265 milligrams

ROASTED GARLIC POTATOES

4 servings/serving size: 4 oz. potatoes

A garlic lovers dream...

- ◆ **1 lb. red potatoes (small to medium ones)**
- ◆ **12 large garlic cloves, peeled and flattened**
- ◆ **2 Tbsp. olive oil**
- ◆ **1/2 tsp. dried rosemary**
- ◆ **Dash salt**
- ◆ **Fresh ground pepper**

1. Wash and clean potatoes. Leave skins on. Cut into wedges, about 1/4-inch thick.
2. In a 13x9x2-inch baking dish, combine potatoes, garlic, oil, and rosemary. Season with salt and pepper and bake at 450 degrees, turning occasionally, for 40 to 45 minutes or until potatoes are tender and crusty. Serve.

Starch/Bread Exchange 1-1/2	Cholesterol .... 0 milligrams
Fat Exchange 1	Total Carbohydrate .... 26 grams
Calories 169	Dietary Fiber .... 2 grams
Total Fat .... 7 grams	Sugars .... 5 grams
Saturated Fat .... 1 gram	Protein .... 3 grams
Calories from Fat 62	Sodium .... 44 milligrams

PARSLEY-STUFFED POTATOES

4 servings/serving size: 1 potato

A good recipe to make for a dinner party. Be sure to use only fresh parsley for this one.

- **4 large baking potatoes (4 to 5 oz. each)**
- **1 Tbsp. olive oil**
- **1 medium onion, chopped**
- **1 cup plain nonfat yogurt**
- **Dash nutmeg**
- **Fresh ground pepper**
- **1/2 cup fresh chopped parsley**
- **1 tsp. salt (optional)**

1. Bake potatoes in a 350-degree oven for 50 to 60 minutes, or until tender when tested with a fork.
2. Heat olive oil in a small skillet, and add onion. Saute onion until tender.
3. Scoop out potatoes (reserve shells). Mash, while still hot, with just enough of the yogurt to make the potatoes light and fluffy. Add nutmeg, pepper, parsley, salt, and sauteed onions to potato mixture.
4. Return potato to shells, and place back in the oven for another 20 to 25 minutes.

....

Starch/Bread Exchange 2-1/2	Total Carbohydrate .... 38 grams
Calories 204	Dietary Fiber .... 4 grams
Total Fat .... 4 grams	Sugars .... 9 grams
Saturated Fat .... 1 gram	Protein .... 6 grams
Calories from Fat 33	Sodium .... 343 milligrams
Cholesterol .... 1 milligram	w/o added salt ...... 52 milligrams

POTATO PARMESAN CHIPS

8 servings/serving size: 1/2 potato

Very tasty and colorful and a change from the usual plain potato.

- ◆ **4 large potatoes (4 to 5 oz. each)**
- ◆ **Nonstick cooking spray**
- ◆ **2 Tbsp. olive oil**
- ◆ **1 tsp. grated onion**
- ◆ **Dash salt**
- ◆ **Fresh ground pepper**
- ◆ **1/4 tsp. paprika**
- ◆ **2 Tbsp. grated Parmesan cheese**

1. Wash and cut unpeeled potatoes into 1/8-inch thick slices. Place in a single layer over baking sheets coated with cooking spray.
2. Heat oil in a small skillet, and add onion, salt, pepper, and paprika. Brush potatoes with oil mixture, and bake at 425 degrees for 15 to 20 minutes or until potatoes are crispy and golden brown.
3. Remove from oven, and sprinkle with cheese. Serve.

....

Starch/Bread Exchange	1	Cholesterol	1 milligram
Fat Exchange	1/2	Total Carbohydrate	16 grams
Calories	105	Dietary Fiber	2 grams
Total Fat	4 grams	Sugars	1 gram
Saturated Fat	1 gram	Protein	2 grams
Calories from Fat	34	Sodium	46 milligrams

HERBED POTATOES

8 servings/serving size: 1 potato

A simple recipe that will impress any guest.

- **8 small to medium red potatoes (2 to 4 oz. each)**
- **4 tsp. fresh minced parsley**
- **2 tsp. fresh minced chives**
- **2 tsp. fresh minced rosemary**
- **1 tsp. fresh minced thyme**
- **1 Tbsp. olive oil**

1. Scrub potatoes, and cut each one in half. Cook, covered, in boiling water for 15 minutes. Drain.
2. In a small roasting pan, toss cooked potatoes with herbs and oil. Bake in a preheated 350-degree oven for 10 minutes until crusty and browned. Serve hot.

....

Starch/Bread Exchange 1	Total Carbohydrate . . . . 17 grams
Calories 88	Dietary Fiber . . . . 2 grams
Total Fat . . . . 2 grams	Sugars . . . . 1 gram
Saturated Fat . . . . 0 grams	Protein . . . . 2 grams
Calories from Fat 16	Sodium . . . . 54 milligrams
Cholesterol . . . . 0 milligrams	

FESTIVE SWEET POTATOES

8 servings/serving size: 1/2 cup

*F*orget gobs of brown sugar and butter. Pineapple and spices add flavor not fat.

- ◆ **4 sweet potatoes (about 20 oz. total)**
- ◆ **2 cups crushed pineapple, in its own juice**
- ◆ **2 tsp. cinnamon**
- ◆ **1 tsp. nutmeg**
- ◆ **Nonstick cooking spray**
- ◆ **1 Tbsp. slivered almonds**

1. In a large saucepan, boil potatoes over medium heat for 45 minutes until you can pierce them easily with a fork (or bake them directly on a rack in a preheated 350-degree oven for 45 minutes).
2. Let potatoes cool, and then gently peel them.
3. Mash potatoes with pineapple and spices, and place in a casserole dish coated with nonstick cooking spray. Top casserole with almonds, and bake for 20 minutes at 350 degrees.

....

Starch/Bread Exchange 1	Total Carbohydrate . . . . 19 grams
Calories 84	Dietary Fiber . . . . 2 grams
Total Fat . . . . 1 gram	Sugars . . . . 11 grams
Saturated Fat . . . . 0 grams	Protein . . . . 1 gram
Calories from Fat 5	Sodium . . . . 7 milligrams
Cholesterol . . . . 0 milligrams	

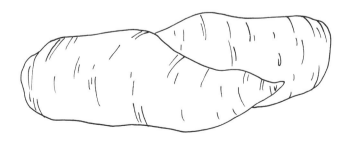

SCALLOPED POTATOES

8 servings/serving size: 1/2 cup

*S*till creamy and rich, but with far less fat.

- ◆ **6 medium potatoes (4 oz. each), unpeeled**
- ◆ **4 cups water**
- ◆ **1 Tbsp. olive oil**
- ◆ **1/3 cup chopped onion**
- ◆ **2 egg substitute equivalents**
- ◆ **1 cup low-fat sour cream**
- ◆ **2 oz. low-fat cheddar cheese, shredded**
- ◆ **Fresh ground pepper**

1. Wash potatoes, and place in a saucepan with water. Bring to a boil, lower the heat, and let potatoes cook for 25 minutes. Drain potatoes, let cool, and slice into 1/4-inch slices.
2. Heat oil in a skillet. Add onion, and saute for 5 minutes. Add onion to egg, sour cream, and pepper in a bowl and mix well.
3. Lay potato slices in a casserole dish. Spoon sour cream mixture over potatoes. Top with cheese.
4. Bake for 35 minutes at 350 degrees until top is browned.

....

Starch/Bread Exchange 1-1/2	Cholesterol .... 2 milligrams
Fat Exchange 1/2	Total Carbohydrate .... 22 grams
Calories 149	Dietary Fiber .... 2 grams
Total Fat .... 4 grams	Sugars .... 6 grams
Saturated Fat .... 2 grams	Protein .... 7 grams
Calories from Fat 39	Sodium .... 108 milligrams

HASH BROWNS

4 servings/serving size: 1/2 cup

*C*rispy potatoes to have anytime.

- ◆ 2 large baking potatoes (about 10 oz. each)
- ◆ 2 Tbsp. minced onion
- ◆ 1 tsp. garlic powder
- ◆ 1/2 tsp. dried thyme
- ◆ Fresh ground pepper
- ◆ Nonstick cooking spray

1. Peel and shred each potato with a hand grater or a food processor with grater attachment. Combine potatoes with onion and spices.
2. Coat a large skillet with cooking spray, and place over medium heat until hot.
3. Pack potato mixture firmly into skillet; cook mixture for 6–8 minutes or until bottom is browned. Invert potato patty onto a plate and return to the skillet, cooked side up.
4. Continue cooking over medium heat for another 6–8 minutes until bottom is browned. Remove from heat and cut into 4 wedges.

. . . .

Starch/Bread Exchange 1-1/2
Calories 100
Total Fat . . . . 0 grams
   Saturated Fat . . . . 0 grams
   Calories from Fat 0
Cholesterol . . . . 0 milligrams

Total Carbohydrate . . . . 23 grams
   Dietary Fiber . . . . 2 grams
   Sugars . . . . 2 grams
Protein . . . . 2 grams
Sodium . . . . 2 grams

SAGE POTATOES

4 servings/serving size: 1/2 potato

A good addition to your brunch table.

- 2 Tbsp. olive oil
- 1 garlic clove, minced
- 1 small onion, chopped
- 1 tsp. dried sage

- 2 potatoes (4 to 5 oz. each), unpeeled, halved lengthwise, and sliced crosswise into thin slices

1. In a large skillet over medium heat, heat oil. Add onion and garlic, and saute for 2 to 3 minutes.
2. Add sage and potatoes and cover and cook for 10 minutes, stirring occasionally. Turn potatoes over using a spatula, and continue to cook for another 5 to 7 minutes until golden brown. Serve.

....

Starch/Bread Exchange	1	Cholesterol	0 milligrams
Fat Exchange	1-1/2	Total Carbohydrate	19 grams
Calories	142	Dietary Fiber	2 grams
Total Fat	7 grams	Sugars	3 grams
Saturated Fat	1 gram	Protein	2 grams
Calories from Fat	62	Sodium	6 milligrams

BAKED POTATO TOPPERS

Try these ideas to spice up your spud! Start by baking an 8-oz. potato for about 50 to 60 minutes in a 350-degree oven.

♦ Create a pizza potato: Add 2 Tbsp. of your favorite tomato sauce and 1 Tbsp. of grated Parmesan cheese. Place potato in oven to melt cheese.

Starch/Bread Exchange 3
Calories 233
Total Fat . . . . 2 grams
  Saturated Fat . . . . 1 gram
  Calories from Fat 16
Cholesterol . . . . 4 milligrams

Total Carbohydrate . . . . 49 grams
  Dietary Fiber . . . . 5 grams
  Sugars . . . . 4 grams
Protein . . . . 7 grams
Sodium . . . . 285 milligrams

♦ Spruce up 1 Tbsp. low-fat sour cream with 1 tsp. chopped chives, thyme, rosemary, or scallions.

Starch/Bread Exchange 3
Calories 222
Total Fat . . . . 1 gram
  Saturated Fat . . . . 1 gram
  Calories from Fat 11
Cholesterol . . . . 0 milligrams

Total Carbohydrate . . . . 48 grams
  Dietary Fiber . . . . 4 grams
  Sugars . . . . 5 grams
Protein . . . . 5 grams
Sodium . . . . 35 milligrams

♦ For more of a main meal, top potatoes with 1/4 cup chopped cooked chicken mixed with 2 Tbsp. salsa.

Starch/Bread Exchange 3
Lean Meat Exchange 1
Calories 278
Total Fat . . . . 2 grams
  Saturated Fat . . . . 0 grams
  Calories from Fat 16

Cholesterol . . . . 36 milligrams
Total Carbohydrate . . . . 48 grams
  Dietary Fiber . . . . 5 grams
  Sugars . . . . 4 grams
Protein . . . . 18 grams
Sodium . . . . 127 milligrams

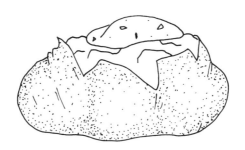

SIDE SALADS

CUCUMBER SALAD WITH YOGURT DRESSING

4 servings/serving size: 1 cup

Top butter lettuce with this dressing for a cool side salad after a spicy meal. You can also use it as a topping for a baked potato.

- ◆ 1/2 cup plain nonfat yogurt
- ◆ 1 Tbsp. dried tarragon or 2 Tbsp. fresh tarragon
- ◆ 2 Tbsp. white wine vinegar
- ◆ 1/4 tsp. dill weed or 1/2 tsp. fresh chopped dill weed
- ◆ 1/4 tsp. cardamom
- ◆ 2 medium cucumbers, peeled, seeded, and diced
- ◆ 5 large radishes, sliced

1. In a small bowl, mix ingredients except vegetables.
2. Just before serving, toss vegetables with the dressing in a medium bowl.

Vegetable Exchange 1
Calories 28
Total Fat . . . . 0 grams
   Saturated Fat . . . . 0 grams
   Calories from Fat 0
Cholesterol . . . . 1 milligram
Total Carbohydrate . . . . 5 grams
   Dietary Fiber . . . . 1 gram
   Sugars . . . . 3 grams
Protein . . . . 2 grams
Sodium . . . . 29 milligrams

TOMATO AND ARTICHOKE SALAD

8 servings/serving size: 1/2 cup

This Italian-flavored salad inspires thick slices of ruby red tomatoes.

- 14-oz. can artichoke hearts, packed in water, drained, and coarsely chopped
- 1/2 cup chopped celery
- 1/4 cup minced scallions
- 1/2 tsp. fresh chopped marjoram or oregano
- 1/4 cup balsamic vinegar
- 2 Tbsp. olive oil
- 1 head butter lettuce, separated into leaves
- 4 medium tomatoes (preferably Beefsteak tomatoes), sliced

1. Combine artichokes, celery, scallions, marjoram, vinegar, and oil. Mix well.
2. Line plates with lettuce. Evenly divide tomatoes over each plate. Place artichoke mixture evenly over tomatoes. Serve.

Vegetable Exchange 1
Fat Exchange 1
Calories 62
Total Fat . . . . 4 grams
  Saturated Fat . . . . 1 gram
  Calories from Fat 35
Cholesterol . . . . 0 milligrams
Total Carbohydrate . . . . 7 grams
  Dietary Fiber . . . . 2 grams
  Sugars . . . . 3 grams
Protein . . . . 2 grams
Sodium . . . . 136 milligrams

ZUCCHINI AND CARROT SALAD*

4 servings/serving size: about 1/2 cup

Julienned ribbons of carrot, zucchini, and fennel in a delightful Dijon vinaigrette.

- 2 medium carrots, peeled and julienned
- 1 medium zucchini, julienned
- 1/2 medium fennel bulb, core removed and julienned
- 1 Tbsp. fresh orange juice
- 2 Tbsp. Dijon mustard
- 3 Tbsp. olive oil
- 1 tsp. white wine vinegar
- 1/2 tsp. dried thyme
- 1 Tbsp. finely minced parsley
- Dash salt
- Fresh ground pepper
- 1/4 cup chopped walnuts
- 1 medium head romaine lettuce, washed and leaves separated

1. Place julienned vegetables in a medium bowl and set aside.
2. Combine remaining ingredients, except walnuts and lettuce, and mix well. Pour dressing over vegetables and toss. Add walnuts and mix again. Refrigerate until ready to serve.
3. To serve, line a bowl or plates with lettuce leaves, and spoon salad on top.

....

Vegetable Exchange	2	Cholesterol	0 milligrams
Fat Exchange	3	Total Carbohydrate	10 grams
Calories	181	Dietary Fiber	5 grams
Total Fat	15 grams	Sugars	4 grams
Saturated Fat	2 grams	Protein	3 grams
Calories from Fat	137	Sodium	155 milligrams

* This recipe is relatively high in fat.

ASPARAGUS WITH VINAIGRETTE

6 servings/serving size: 1/2 cup

The secret to great asparagus is to cook it until it is still bright green and slightly crunchy. Look for thin asparagus with compact buds.

- 1-1/2 lb. fresh or frozen asparagus
- 1/2 cup red wine vinegar
- 1/2 tsp. dried or 1 tsp. fresh tarragon
- 2 Tbsp. fresh chives
- 3 Tbsp. fresh chopped parsley
- 1/2 cup water
- 1 Tbsp. olive oil
- 2 Tbsp. Dijon mustard
- 1 lb. fresh spinach leaves, trimmed of stems, washed, and dried
- 2 large tomatoes, cut in wedges

1. Place 1 inch of water in a pot, and place steamer inside. Arrange asparagus on top of steamer. Steam fresh asparagus for 4 minutes and frozen asparagus for 6 to 8 minutes. Immediately rinse asparagus under cold water to stop the cooking. (This helps keep asparagus bright green and crunchy.) Set aside.
2. In a small bowl or salad cruet, combine remaining ingredients except spinach and tomatoes. Mix or shake well.
3. Pour dressing over asparagus and refrigerate for 5 to 6 hours.
4. To serve, line plates with spinach leaves, and place asparagus on top of spinach. Garnish with tomato wedges, and spoon any remaining dressing on top.

....

Vegetable Exchange	. . . .	2
Fat Exchange	. . . .	1/2
Calories	. . . .	68
Total Fat	. . . .	3 grams
Saturated Fat	. . . .	0 grams
Calories from Fat	. . . .	28

Cholesterol	. . . .	0 milligrams
Total Carbohydrate	. . . .	9 grams
Dietary Fiber	. . . .	4 grams
Sugars	. . . .	4 grams
Protein	. . . .	4 grams
Sodium	. . . .	127 milligrams

SPINACH AND MUSHROOM SALAD

6 servings/serving size: 1/2 cup

The warm dressing on this salad makes it special.

- ◆ **1 lb. spinach leaves, stems trimmed, washed, and dried**
- ◆ **1/2 lb. sliced fresh mushrooms**
- ◆ **1 red onion, sliced into thin rings**
- ◆ **1/4 cup mandarin oranges**

- ◆ **1/4 cup red wine vinegar**
- ◆ **2 Tbsp. lite soy sauce**
- ◆ **2 tsp. olive oil**
- ◆ **1 garlic clove, minced**
- ◆ **Fresh ground pepper**

1. In a large salad bowl, combine spinach, mushrooms, onion, and oranges.
2. In a small saucepan, combine remaining ingredients. Bring to a boil, and then pour over salad. Serve immediately.

....

Vegetable Exchange 2	Total Carbohydrate . . . . 9 grams
Calories 44	Dietary Fiber . . . . 3 grams
Total Fat . . . . 0 grams	Sugars . . . . 4 grams
Saturated Fat . . . . 0 grams	Protein . . . . 3 grams
Calories from Fat 0	Sodium . . . . 264 milligrams
Cholesterol . . . . 0 milligrams	

GREEN BEAN AND ENDIVE SALAD

2 servings/serving size: 1 cup

Add zip to Boston lettuce by combining it with endive, green beans, and red pepper. A nice salad for picnics.

- 6 oz. green beans, trimmed and cut into 1-inch pieces
- 1 large head Belgian endive, cut crosswise into 1-inch pieces
- 1/2 small head Boston lettuce, torn into bite-sized pieces
- 1 red pepper, chopped
- 1-1/2 tsp. lemon juice
- 1-1/2 tsp. Dijon mustard
- 1 tsp. dried basil or 2 tsp. fresh chopped basil
- 1-1/2 Tbsp. olive oil
- 1 Tbsp. low-sodium chicken broth
- Dash salt (optional)
- Fresh ground pepper

1. Boil or microwave green beans until just tender. Drain and run cool water over the beans to keep them bright green and crunchy.
2. Combine cooled beans with endive, Boston lettuce, and red pepper.
3. In a small bowl, whisk together lemon juice, mustard, and basil. Slowly add oil and broth, and blend well. Season with salt and pepper.
4. Pour dressing over the salad, toss, and refrigerate. Serve cold.

....

Vegetable Exchange 2	Total Carbohydrate . . . . 12 grams
Fat Exchange 2	Dietary Fiber . . . . 6 grams
Calories 149	Sugars . . . . 3 grams
Total Fat . . . . 11 grams	Protein . . . . 3 grams
Saturated Fat . . . . 1 gram	Sodium . . . . 144 milligrams
Calories from Fat 99	w/o added salt . . . . . . 74 milligrams
Cholesterol . . . . 0 milligrams	

OVERNIGHT COLESLAW

6 servings/serving size: about 1 cup

This salad gets all its flavor from spices and apple juice instead of high-fat mayonnaise.

- 4 cups shredded cabbage (green or purple or a mixture)
- 2 cup shredded carrots
- 3/4 cup sliced scallions
- 3/4 cup unsweetened apple juice
- 2/3 cup cider vinegar
- 1-1/2 tsp. paprika
- 1 tsp. mustard seeds
- 1/2 tsp. garlic powder
- 1/2 tsp. celery seeds
- Fresh ground pepper
- 1 Tbsp. dry mustard

1. Combine cabbage, carrots, and scallions.
2. Combine remaining ingredients in a blender, and pour over cabbage mixture. Toss to coat. Refrigerate overnight, and serve chilled.

....

Vegetable Exchange 2
Calories 47
Total Fat . . . . 0 grams
  Saturated Fat . . . . 0 grams
  Calories from Fat 0
Cholesterol . . . . 0 milligrams
Total Carbohydrate . . . . 12 grams
  Dietary Fiber . . . . 2 grams
  Sugars . . . . 9 grams
Protein . . . . 1 gram
Sodium . . . . 22 milligrams

PEAR AND BLUE CHEESE SALAD

4 servings/serving size: 1/2 cup

Serve this festive side salad during a favorite holiday.

- **1 small head butter lettuce, torn into bite-sized pieces**
- **1/2 lb. watercress leaves**
- **2 large pears** (red D'Anjou are nice), **cored and cut into eighths**
- **1/3 cup crumbled blue cheese**

- **2 Tbsp. olive oil**
- **1/3 cup lemon juice**
- **1 large shallot, minced**
- **Fresh ground pepper**
- **4 tsp. chopped walnuts to garnish**

1. In a large bowl, combine lettuce and watercress. Arrange greens on individual plates.
2. Place pear halves in a circular pattern over greens. Top each salad with cheese.
3. In a jar, combine oil, lemon juice, shallot, and pepper. Shake well, and pour over each salad. Garnish with walnuts.

. . . .

Vegetable Exchange	1	Cholesterol	7 milligrams
Fruit Exchange	1	Total Carbohydrate	20 grams
Fat Exchange	2	Dietary Fiber	4 grams
Calories	185	Sugars	15 grams
Total Fat	11 grams	Protein	4 grams
Saturated Fat	3 grams	Sodium	151 milligrams
Calories from Fat	101		

INDEX

DIG INTO OUR *RECIPE-PACKED PANTRY OF COOKBOOKS AND MENU PLANNERS*

Healthy Selects: Spark Plugs for Your Taste Buds

Dozens of recipes were chosen for each *Healthy Selects* cookbook, but only the 60 most tempting were chosen. Every recipe will fit nicely into your healthy meal plan. Calories, fats, sodium, carbohydrates, cholesterol counts, and food exchanges accompany every recipe.

♦ **GREAT STARTS & FINE FINISHES**

Now you can begin every dinner with an enticing appetizer and finish it off with a "now I'm REALLY satisfied" dessert. Choose from recipes like Crab-Filled Mushrooms, Broiled Shrimp with Garlic, Baked Scallops, Creamy Tarragon Dip, or Cheesy Tortilla Wedges to start; serve Cherry Cobbler, Fresh Apple Pie, Cherry Cheesecake, Chocolate Cupcakes, or dozens of others to finish. Softcover. #CCBGSFF
Nonmember: $8.95/Member: $7.15

♦ **EASY & ELEGANT ENTREES**

Tired of leaving the dinner table feeling like you've had nothing more than a snack? Pull up a chair to *Easy & Elegant Entrees*. Now you can sit down to Fettucine with Peppers and Broccoli, Steak with Brandied Onions, Shrimp Creole, and dozens of others. They taste like they took hours to prepare, but you can put them on the table in minutes. Softcover. #CCBEEE
Nonmember: $8.95/Member: $7.15

♦ **SAVORY SOUPS & SALADS**

When your meals need a little something extra, or you just want something light, invite *Savory Soups & Salads* to lunch and dinner. They just might become your favorite guests. Choose from Pasta-Stuffed Tomato Salad, Mediterranean Chicken Salad, Hot Clam Chowder, Cool Gazpacho, and more. Softcover. #CCBSSS
Nonmember: $8.95/Member: $7.15

♦ **QUICK & HEARTY MAIN DISHES**

When you're looking for simple, great-tasting meals but can't quite find the time, it's time for *Quick & Hearty Main Dishes*. You'll find Apple Cinnamon Pork Chops, Beef Stroganoff, Broiled Salmon Steaks, Spicy Chicken Drumsticks, Almond Chicken, and many others. Softcover. #CCBQHMD
Nonmember: $8.95/Member: $7.15

♦ **SIMPLE & TASTY SIDE DISHES**

Softcover. #CCBSTSD. *Nonmember: $8.95/Member: $7.15*

The *Month of Meals* series:
Automatic meal planning with a turn of the page

Each *Month of Meals* menu planner offers 28 days' worth of fresh new menu choices. The pages are split into thirds and interchangeable, so you can flip to any combination of breakfast, lunch, and dinner. So no matter which combinations you choose, your nutrients and exchanges will still be correct for the entire day—automatically!

◆ **MONTH OF MEALS**

Choose from Chicken Cacciatore, Oven Fried Fish, Sloppy Joes, Crab Cakes, many others. Spiral-bound. #CMPMOM
Nonmember: $12.50/Member: $9.95

◆ **MONTH OF MEALS 2**

Month of Meals 2 features tips and meal suggestions for Mexican, Italian, and Chinese restaurants. Menu choices include Beef Burritos, Chop Suey, Veal Piccata, Stuffed Peppers, many others. Spiral-bound. #CMPMOM2
Nonmember: $12.50/Member: $9.95

◆ **MONTH OF MEALS 3**

How long has it been since you could eat fast food without guilt? Now you can—*Month of Meals 3* shows you how. Choose from McDonald's, Wendy's, Taco Bell, and others. Menu choices include Kentucky Fried Chicken, Stouffer's Macaroni and Cheese, Fajita in a Pita, Seafood Stir-Fry, others. Spiral-bound. #CMPMOM3
Nonmember: $12.50/Member: $9.95

◆ **MONTH OF MEALS 4**

Beef up your meal planning with our "meat and potatoes" menu planner. Menu options include Oven Crispy Chicken, Beef Stroganoff, Cornbread Pie, many others. Spiral-bound. #CMPMOM4
Nonmember: $12.50/Member: $9.95

◆ **MONTH OF MEALS 5**

Automatic meal planning goes vegetarian! Choose from a garden of fresh selections like Eggplant Italian, Stuffed Zucchini, Cucumbers with Dill Dressing, Vegetable Lasagna, many others. Spiral-bound. #CMPMOM5
Nonmember: $12.50/Member: $9.95

◆ **HEALTHY HOMESTYLE COOKBOOK**

Choose from more than 150 healthy new recipes with old-fashioned great taste. Just like grandma used to make—but **without** all that fat. Complete nutrition information—calories, protein, fat, fiber, saturated fat, sodium, cholesterol, carbohydrate counts, and diabetic exchanges—accompanies every recipe. Special introductory section features "how-to" cooking tips, plus energy- and time-saving tips for microwaving. Lay-flat binding allows hands-free reference to any recipe. Softcover. #CCBHHS
Nonmember: $12.50/Member: $9.95

☐ **YES!** Please send me the following books:

Book Name: _____ Quantity: _____
Item Number: _____ Total: _____
Price Each: _____

Book Name: _____ Quantity: _____
Item Number: _____ Total: _____
Price Each: _____

Book Name: _____ Quantity: _____
Item Number: _____ Total: _____
Price Each: _____

Book Name: _____ Quantity: _____
Item Number: _____ Total: _____
Price Each: _____

Publications Subtotal $ _____
Virginia residents add 4.5% state sales tax $ _____
Add shipping & handling (see chart) $ _____
Add $15 for each international shipment $ _____
GRAND TOTAL $ _____

Name _____

Address _____

City/State/Zip _____

☐ Payment enclosed (check or money order)
☐ Charge my: ☐ VISA ☐ MasterCard ☐ American Express

Account Number _____

Signature _____

Exp. Date _____   CHA95HS

Shipping & Handling
Up to $30 . . . . .add $3.00
$30.01-$50 . . . . .add $4.00
Over $50 . . . . .add 8%

Mail to: American Diabetes Association
          1970 Chain Bridge Road
          McLean, VA 22109-0592

Allow 2-3 weeks for shipment. Add $3 for each extra shipping
address. Prices subject to change without notice. Foreign orders
must be paid in U.S. funds, drawn on a U.S. bank.